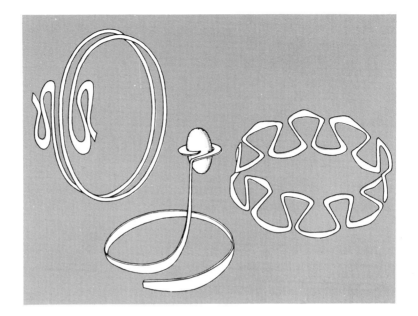

**LITTLE CRAFT
BOOK SERIES**

Make Your Own ELEGANT JEWELRY

By R. Boulay

STERLING PUBLISHING CO., Inc., New York
SAUNDERS OF TORONTO, Ltd.,   Don Mills, Canada

Oak Tree Press Co., Ltd.
London & Sydney

Little Craft Book Series

Translated by Manly Banister
Adapted by Anne E. Kallem

Front cover photograph by Bijoux Galerie, Paris, France

The original edition was published in France under the title, "Créez Vos Bijoux,"
© 1970 by Bordas, Paris, France.

Copyright © 1972 by Sterling Publishing Co., Inc.
419 Park Avenue South, New York, N.Y. 10016
Distributed in Canada by Saunders of Toronto, Ltd., Don Mills, Ontario
British edition published by Oak Tree Press Co., Ltd., Nassau, Bahamas
Distributed in Australia by Oak Tree Press Co., Ltd.,
P.O. Box 34, Brickfield Hill, Sydney 2000, N.S.W.
Distributed in the United Kingdom and elsewhere in the British Commonwealth
by Ward Lock Ltd., 116 Baker Street, London W 1
Manufactured in the United States of America
All rights reserved
Library of Congress Catalog Card No.: 72-81042
ISBN 0-8069-5222-9   UK 7061 2380-8
5223-7

Contents

Before You Begin

Elegant jewelry no longer conjures up in people's minds just the Crown Jewels or Tiffany's window! Today, elegance implies simplicity, cleanness of design, and above all—the personal touch of the individual who wears it. And what could be more individual than jewelry conceived by *you* and turned out by your own hands!

Here on these pages is everything that you need to know about the basic techniques for making marvellous metal jewelry of *your own design*. This book is unique in that it doesn't dictate to you *what* you should make. It simply gives you the tools and techniques to exercise your own creativity and imagination, and allows you to make jewelry that is your very own personal expression. The finished jewelry that is shown in the photographs stand merely for examples of what you can do when you learn the techniques in this book.

All of the materials and tools used are easily acquired from hobby shops and craft supply houses. Beginner's jewelry kits are available which include all the equipment you will need for almost every process from soldering to mounting your finished pieces. The initial investment is actually small when you consider what you are going to produce in the way of genuinely unique and beautiful jewelry.

The book is divided up into two general sections, one dealing with techniques for working with wire and rods and the other for working with

Illus. 1.

sheet metal. All of the metals suggested are inexpensive and easily worked. Naturally, you will want to combine wires and sheets, but it is wise first to learn the various methods and tools required for each type of metal.

Once you have made your first spirals, curves, and bangle earrings, there will be no stopping you! So now, *Begin.*

Wires and Rods

You can create truly elegant pieces of jewelry out of simple metal wire and rods, cutting and shaping them to suit the compositions of your own designs for rings, chains, earrings, settings, clasps, and so on.

You will be using non-ferrous wires or rods made of copper (red), brass (yellow), and nickel-silver (white), which is also called German silver.

The metal can be hammer-hardened, as in the case of nickel-silver, or softened by annealing, as with copper and brass.

Wires and rods are available either round or square; however, to begin, you will be wise to use round wire. Wire is made in a variety of thicknesses which are expressed in terms of the Brown-and-Sharpe gauge system. For most of your jewelry, 20 gauge, 18 gauge, 16 gauge and 14 gauge will be most suitable. The higher the gauge number, the lighter, or thinner, the wire. Therefore, any wire that is 12 gauge or heavier is considered a rod. (The corresponding diameters are as follows: 20 gauge = .0320″; 18 gauge = .0403″; 16 gauge = .0508″; 14 gauge = .0641″; 12 gauge = .0808″.)

Designing

The first step is sketching the design of your chosen piece of jewelry on paper before you set to work to produce it. Keep your drawing simple and remember that a piece of metal is not as obliging as a pencil line. For sketching out your designs you will need paper, pencil, eraser, graduated ruler, carbon paper, and white cardboard.

Wherever wires cross, they create extra thickness that you must consider. Keep in mind the solidity of the piece as well as the outline. Also, the places where pieces are soldered together will add to the strength and stability of the design.

Trace the design from your paper onto white cardboard, using carbon paper. The cardboard must be thick enough not to frazzle on the edges when you use it as a guide for bending wires.

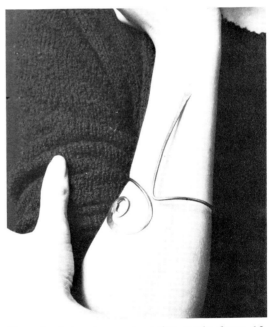

Illus. 2. A handsome bracelet made from 16-gauge square brass wire. Care must be taken when working with square wire because when it is shaped, the bending so deforms the wire it cannot be re-done.

5

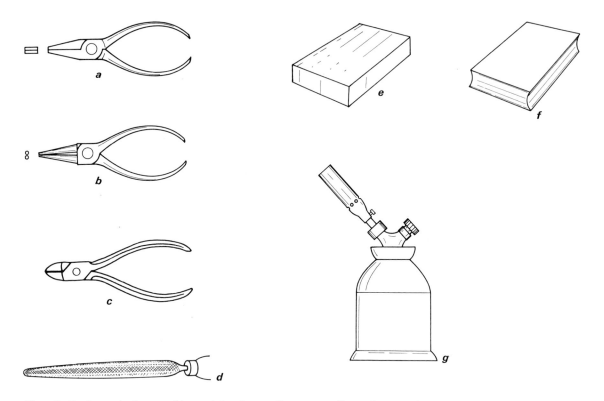

Illus. 3. Basic tools for working with wire. *a.* flat-nose pliers. *b.* round-nose pliers. *c.* diagonal wire cutters. *d.* file. *e.* wooden bench block. *f.* bench anvil. *g.* propane gas torch.

Shaping Curves and Angles

Tools and Materials: Wire. String or copper wire on a spool. Diagonal wire cutters. Semi-fine file. Round-nose pliers. Flat-nose pliers. Bench block (made of rock maple or Brazilian rosewood). Steel bench anvil. Propane gas torch which adjusts from a needlepoint flame to a bush.

Measuring Wire

You cannot measure while handling a whole roll of wire. When cutting off a piece of wire by eye, you can make a mistake and cut the piece too short for the project; or, you can cut it too long and waste your material.

The best thing is to lay, right on the drawing, a

length of thin, pliable, copper wire or a piece of string which will unroll and roll up easily and allow you to measure the length of each piece with precision.

Cut the measured wire off with an inch or more to spare (for safety's sake), using the diagonal wire cutters. Then file the sharp ends smooth with a semi-fine file.

From time to time, refer to the drawing (Illus. 4). If you are working on several identical pieces at the same time, compare them, not only with the original design, but also with each other.

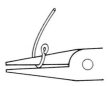

Illus. 5. Making tight curves with the pliers.

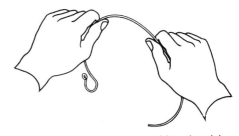

Illus. 6. Making large curves and bends with your hands.

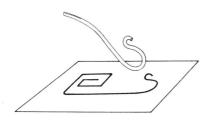

Illus. 4. From time to time check your work against the design.

Working with Pliers

Tight curves are made with the point of the round-nose pliers, and large curves are made with the base of the jaws of the same pliers (Illus. 5). Long, graceful curves are best made with your fingers (Illus. 6).

You can bend wire at a right angle between the jaws of the flat-nose pliers by bending it down while pulling it over either the thin end or the thicker base of the jaws (Illus. 7).

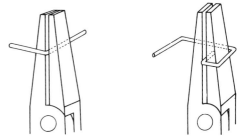

Illus. 7. Forming right angles with the aid of the pliers.

7

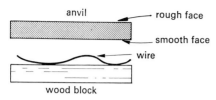

anvil
rough face
smooth face
wire
wood block

Illus. 8. Flattening wire.

anneal them several times to make them malleable enough to work with.

Shaping a Simple Loop

You will need the same materials as on page 6.

Begin by bending the end of the wire back upon itself with the round-nose pliers (Illus. 10).

Flattening Wire

When you curve a wire gracefully, you are actually twisting it in three dimensions. You can easily flatten the *shape* by squeezing it between two blocks of wood, or an anvil and one block of wood (Illus. 8). You must always use at least one wood block, because this allows the wire to keep its shape. If two metal blocks are used, the wire itself is so flattened it is made unusable.

Annealing Wire

A wire that has been bent and straightened too many times becomes hard and brittle. It must be annealed by heating it red-hot with the propane gas torch, and then dipping the piece into water to cool it. (Use copper tongs for this purpose.) You must always anneal brass wire before working it.

Rods (wire over 12 gauge) cannot be bent as easily as the lighter weight wire. You will have to

Illus. 9. A looped earring made from hammer-hardened nickel-silver wire. Tiny twists of wire tie the loops together.

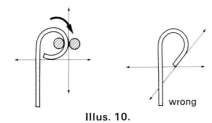

Illus. 10.

You must bend it into a circle, not an oval (Illus. 10). Proceed with a succession of small twists with the pliers; then bring back into the axis of the

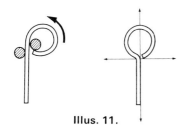

Illus. 11.

wire the loop which was first formed off to one side (Illus. 11).

Little eyelets such as these are very important in making pieces composed of links or clasps.

Shaping a Spiral

Tools and Materials: Same as on page 6, plus: Wooden tool handle with rounded end (or a large dowel). Nail with the head cut off. Hand drill. Hammer. Bench vice.

Drive a headless nail into the middle of the rounded end of a wooden tool handle. Use a 3d

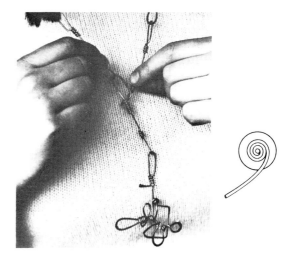

Illus. 12. A necklace made of nickel-silver, bent, hammered and spiralled.

(three-penny) or 4d nail, leaving about $\frac{1}{4}''$ sticking out at the top (Illus. 13).

Right next to the nail, drill a hole, having the same diameter as the wire, to a $\frac{3}{8}''$ depth. Grip the handle in a vice, with the rounded end up. Slip the end of the wire into the hole and wrap it tightly round the nail, then round each turn of wire as it is laid down.

After removing the finished spiral, cut off the inside end, which will be sticking up.

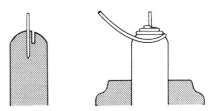

Illus. 13. Shaping a spiral.

9

Shaping a Series of Loops

Tools and Materials: Same as before, plus: Strong board or piece of thick plywood. Some 8d or 10d nails with the heads cut off. Hammer.

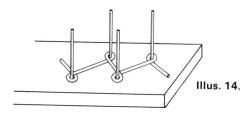

Illus. 14.

Lay out the pattern for the bending device in pencil on a piece of wood in accordance with the measurements of your design. Drive headless nails into the board as shown in Illus. 14, spacing them as on the design. Twist the wire back and forth round the nails in the pattern as shown in Illus. 14.

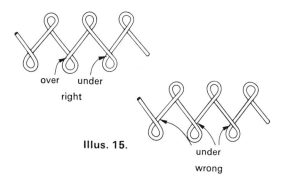

over   under
right

Illus. 15.

under
wrong

To avoid having the same lines always on top or underneath, which would make a piece of jewelry too thick, *alternate the crossing* of the wires, over and under, as shown in Illus. 15.

10

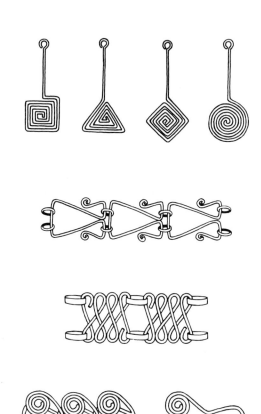

Illus. 16. Elements in earrings, bracelets, and necklaces made from shaped, looped and spiralled wire.

Shaping Wire Jump Rings

Tools and Materials: Wire of whatever gauge desired. A small rod having same diameter as the wire. Hand drill. Bench vice. Jeweler's hacksaw.

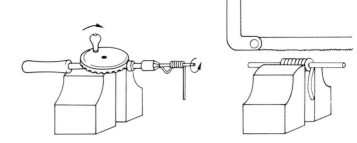

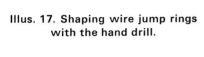

Illus. 17. Shaping wire jump rings with the hand drill.

Take a round, square, or oval rod, according to the size and shape of the desired rings. Insert the rod in the chuck of the hand drill along with the end of the wire chosen for the rings. Grip the drill in a bench vice so that the turning handle is on top (Illus. 17). Turn this with one hand while, with the other, guide the wire as it wraps round the rod.

Remove the rod and the wrapped-around wire from the drill chuck and grip them in the bench vice. Saw the turned wire parallel to the rod with the hacksaw. When released from the vice, the "turns" fall apart, each becoming a ring. Be sure that you hold the saw vertical so that the kerf (cut) will be clean and narrow. If the wire is fine, it is preferable to remove the rings from the rod and cut them apart one at a time with the diagonal cutters, following a straight line down the row of turns.

After cutting, file the ends of the rings off square. They can be soldered together when needed (see page 16).

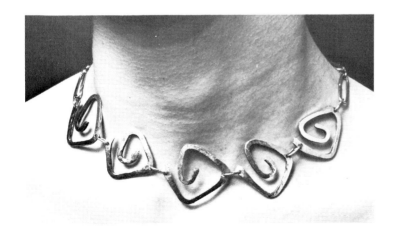

Illus. 18. Wire jump rings connect the various pieces of this 18-gauge nickel-silver wire necklace.

Hammering Wire and Rod

Tools and Materials: Steel bench anvil. 2 C-clamps (optional). Dapping punch. Ball-peen hammer. Planishing hammer. Propane gas torch.

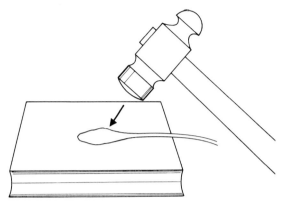

Illus. 20. Hammering the end of a piece of wire.

Hammering the End

Place the end of the wire on a bench anvil or a $\frac{3}{4}''$-thick plate of cold rolled steel. Holding it with one hand, strike the piece with the flat face of the planishing hammer, inclining the hammer head

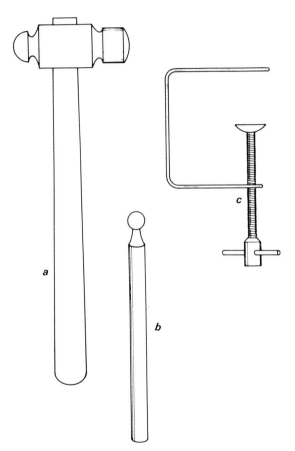

Illus. 19. Tools for hammering wire and rod. *a*. hammer. *b*. dapping punch. *c*. C-clamp.

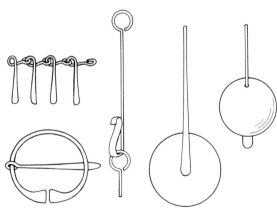

Illus. 21. Some applications of hammered ends.

Illus. 22. A simple necklace made of 18-gauge nickel-silver wire which has been hammered, flattened on the ends, and shaped.

at such an angle that the blow tends to push the metal towards the end of the wire, and not the

other way, that is, towards the body of the wire (Illus. 20).

Continue hammering with light, successive strokes. Try to keep the surface as smooth as possible, avoiding rough "ledges" marking each separate stroke.

This technique is used to keep a bead from slipping off the end of a wire (the hammered part is smoothed down to make it invisible). It is also used for clasps, as you will see later on. Also, it provides a better hold when you are soldering wire to a flat surface. Decorative effects can be obtained when the flattened end is then shaped with a file.

Illus. 23. Here, a decorative touch is added in the form of a flattened end which has been shaped with a file.

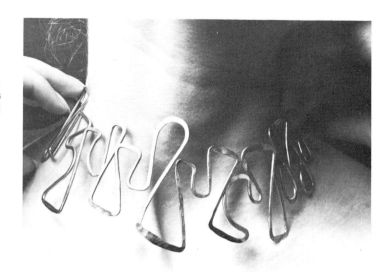

Illus. 24. A necklace made of 20-gauge nickel-silver wire which was first annealed, and then shaped and hammered.

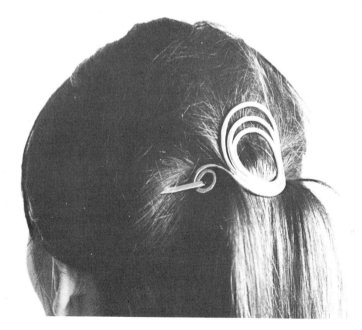

Illus. 25. A barrette made of 18-gauge brass wire which was hammered and shaped.

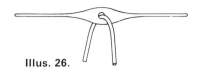

Illus. 26.

Hammering Flats in Wire

A flat is a small, flat spot within the length of a wire, hammered in for decorative purposes or to provide a place for drilling through the wire.

You can clamp the wire to the bench anvil with a pair of C-clamps if you have them, or simply hold it by hand. Place the ball end of a dapping punch on the wire where you want the flat, and strike it with a precisely vertical blow of the hammer to avoid skidding. If you do not have a dapping punch, a good substitute is the ball side of a ball-peen hammer. Strike the wire directly with it (if you're very adept at hammering), or hold it with the ball against the wire and hit the

flat face with another hammer. Avoid thinning the metal too much, as this makes it fragile.

This little trick is used particularly to isolate a bead on a wire or, as mentioned before, to provide a space for piercing the wire (Illus. 26).

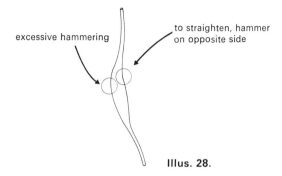

excessive hammering

to straighten, hammer on opposite side

Illus. 28.

Over-all Hammering

You may want to hammer a wire its full length to make a wire ribbon of it, or to flatten a piece that has already been shaped. Use the flat face of the hammer, holding the work firmly in place on the anvil. To straighten the metal in the course of hammering, always, after striking one of the sides of the wire for a while, turn it over and strike the other side in exactly the same place with exactly the same force (Illus. 27).

If the metal becomes too hard after a few hammer blows, you will have to anneal it (page 8). Annealing is especially necessary, as mentioned earlier, for brass.

When you want to flatten a piece that has already been shaped, be particularly careful working the bent parts where you will have to adjust the force of your blows to the condition of the wire.

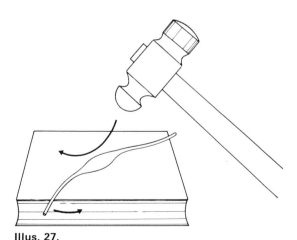

Illus. 27.

15

Soldering

Illus. 29. Soldering alone permits you to create designs such as these.

Soldering is the process of joining two pieces of metal by means of the fusion of a third metal. There are two basic soldering procedures—one using tin solder (*soft soldering*); the other using silver solder (*hard soldering*).

Soft soldering is especially useful for attaching such things as pins, cuff-link findings, or earring findings. Silver soldering, which is performed at a temperature considerably hotter than that required for soft soldering, is used for all other kinds of assembly (wire to metal plate, wire to wire, and so on). Silver soldering provides a much harder and more tenacious hold, and it makes it easier for you to do a cleaner, more successful soldering job than does tin soldering.

16

Soft Soldering

Tools and Materials: Emery cloth. Soft, clean dry cloth. Soldering paste for non-ferrous metals. Clear brushing lacquer (or clear nail polish), and a No. 1 or No. 2 camel's-hair or red sable brush. Sheet of hard asbestos or a firebrick (insulating brick). Blocks. C-clamps. Pliers. Spool of 50–50 soft solder (50% tin and 50% lead). Propane gas torch with adjustable flame from needlepoint to bush. Semi-fine file. Hollow scraper. Special cleaning solution for spots and traces of solder. Also handy for delicate objects is an electric soldering iron (at *least* 80 watts).

Cleaning

First, carefully rub with emery cloth those surfaces which are to figure in the assembly, so that the bare metal is exposed. Complete the cleaning by wiping hard with a dry rag. From here on, take special care not to touch the parts involved with your bare fingertips, which contain oil. Spread a layer of soldering paste over the surfaces to be soldered, apply a coat of clear brushing lacquer, and let dry. This will be burned up in the course of tinning the piece, but it will, at the same time, keep the solder from flowing where it is not wanted. The pieces are now ready for tinning.

Tinning

Tinning consists of covering the surfaces to be joined with a thin film of solder. If ordinary solid tin solder is used, you have to use it together with a flux, such as rosin, which is applied to the metal just before soldering. It cleans and frees the metal

Illus. 30. Cleaning the metal.

Illus. 31. Applying soldering paste.

Illus. 32. Lacquering.

17

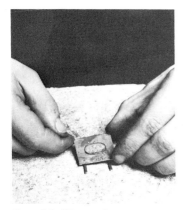

Illus. 33. Place piece on support.

Illus. 34. Heating with soldering iron.

Illus. 35. Heating with propane torch.

surfaces of oxide and thus promotes fusion. Solder will not flow over an oxidized surface.

Place the prepared pieces on your asbestos pad or on a firebrick. If you are soldering pieces over

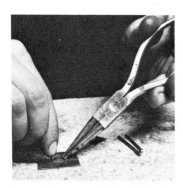

Illus. 36. Placing the piece to be soldered, using pliers.

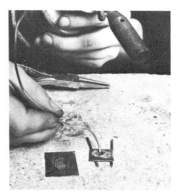

Illus. 37. Applying soft solder.

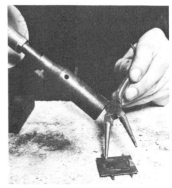

Illus. 38. Final soldering.

18

$2\frac{1}{2}''$, you must avoid waste of heat caused by conduction. To do this, place a little support, no more than $\frac{1}{8}''$ high, between the asbestos pad and the metal. It must present the smallest surface possible to the workpiece (Illus. 33).

If the pieces are of good size, heat them with the propane torch (Illus. 35). Smaller pieces, such as the wire jump rings, can be heated with a soldering iron (Illus. 34).

Before a piece gets red hot, remove the flame or soldering iron and touch the end of the wire solder to the hot piece. If the temperature of the metal is high enough, the solder will melt on contact and flow out over the surface. If it was not heated enough, the solder may still melt, but it will form a granular cake. In this case, turn the flame back on the piece, or touch it again with the soldering iron, until the solder spreads out in a shiny layer. Remove the source of heat at once in order not to damage the strength of the solder by excessive heat.

Take note! A thin film of solder is enough. Too thick a layer will only jeopardize the soldering job. If you get too much solder on, re-heat until the solder flows well; then at once quickly wipe the surface with a rag. This will pick up the surplus solder.

Remember, the parts to be joined must reach the melting point of the solder at the same time. It is never the flame or the soldering iron that

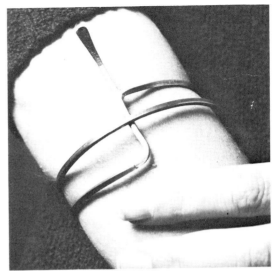

Illus. 39. An elegant bracelet created by soldering.

Illus. 40. Each "V" shape in this brooch is made of 20-gauge, hammer-hardened, and shaped nickel-silver wire with the ends flattened. The pieces were then soldered together to form a flowerlike effect.

19

Designs that can be realized only by soldering are shown on these two pages.

melts the solder, but the metal itself, which has been charged with heat from the source.

When the tinned pieces have cooled, examine them to make sure that they are ready for the actual soldering, or joining.

The solder should look glossy and brilliant. This is an opportune time to renew the lacquer which was burned by the flame.

Now you must place in close contact the surfaces you are going to solder together. In soldering flat work, you do not need a holding device for the parts to be joined. Where you do need such a device, however, you can use a vice, or jam the parts between bricks. The important thing is to avoid large losses of heat caused by contact with a large, heat-conducting surface.

When the different pieces are all set, heat them all at once, either with the torch or with the soldering iron, concentrating the source of heat towards the thickest and largest piece. The solder melts rapidly and shines brilliantly. Remove the flame immediately and let the work cool for several minutes, watching to see that the surfaces

being soldered together continue to be pressed tightly against each other.

There is nothing more to do except clean the metal by removing all traces of oxidation with emery cloth or a hollow scraper, as well as the spots of burned lacquer and the excess solder. (Never use a file for this purpose. Once solder gets into a file, it cannot be removed.)

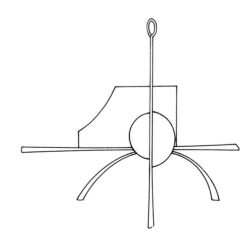

Illus. 41. Fluxing the metal.

Illus. 42. Putting the pieces into position.

Illus. 43. Heating with the torch.

Illus. 44. Applying the silver solder.

Hard Soldering

Tools and Materials: Emery cloth. Clean, soft, dry rag. Flux for hard solder. Sheet of hard asbestos. Pliers. C-clamps. Some brazing rods or wire of silver solder. Propane gas torch. File. Hollow scraper.

The silver solder or brazing compound should flow and penetrate, by capillary action, the joint between the two pieces being soldered. This means that the metal sheets must be perfectly flat, and the ends of wires very straight. There must be no spaces between the joining surfaces. If there are, eliminate them first by filing.

Cleaning

As for soft soldering, scrape the metal bare with emery cloth or a file, and wipe with a rag, avoiding any contact with your fingers, as they are always a little greasy.

Next, brush on a layer of flux. This is sometimes available in a liquid form. After fluxing, the pieces are ready to be silver-soldered together.

Soldering

Place all of the pieces to be assembled in position. Make sure the set-up is very stable and arranged so as to avoid large losses of heat by conduction. Light the torch and begin by heating the largest pieces. At the precise moment when the entire assembly is glowing cherry red (a very bright red), carefully touch the rod or wire of silver solder to the soldering point.

If the piece is at the right temperature, the hard solder liquefies immediately and is drawn by capillary action between the two pieces joined together. Take care to remove the silver solder immediately after the touch, to avoid over-running the piece with solder.

Allow the flame to heat the piece for a few seconds longer; then, take it away. Wait a minute longer, and then cool the piece quickly by plunging it into water. Next, with emery cloth and scraper, clean away all traces of oxidation and excess solder.

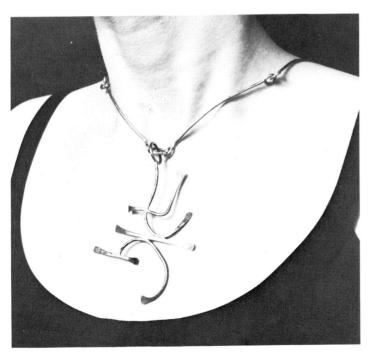

Illus. 45. A necklace of 18-gauge nickel-silver wire with a pendant of the same wire, flattened on the ends and soldered together.

23

Sheet Metals

The different techniques involved in making jewelry from sheet metal can be grouped as follows:

(1) Tracing, cutting out, filing and piercing; (2) shaping; (3) surfacing—chasing and etching; (4) riveting; (5) finishing—cleaning, polishing, applying a patina, and mounting.

For making jewelry with sheet metal, you will again be using the following metals—copper, brass, and nickel-silver—plus zinc. Copper, brass, and nickel-silver sheets are available both hammer-hardened and annealed. The annealed metal is more malleable, but its appearance tends to be less attractive. Copper, brass, and zinc are easy to work; nickel-silver is somewhat more difficult because it is harder.

Sheet metal comes in the same Brown-and-Sharpe gauge measurements as wire. Remember to choose only non-ferrous metals to work with.

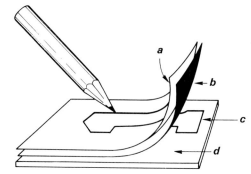

Illus. 47. Tracing the design. *a.* drawing. *b.* carbon paper. *c.* tracing on the metal. *d.* metal.

Designing

You will need paper, pencil, eraser, graduated ruler and carbon paper. In addition, you will need a tracing point, a steel square, and a pair of dividers. Since almost all jewelry meant to be worn is rather small, avoid forms that are too complex, particularly any involving very sharp angles which might look beautiful on paper, but which will present considerable difficulty in working on the metal itself.

When you have made a clear drawing of the design on the scale you wish it, and all the techniques involved are clear in your mind, transfer the outline to the piece of metal in preparation for cutting out.

To do this, slip a sheet of carbon paper between the drawing and metal surface; then go over the lines of the drawing with a sharp pencil (Illus. 46). The carbon drawing on the metal will next have to be gone over lightly with a tracing point or metal scriber so the lines cannot be rubbed off.

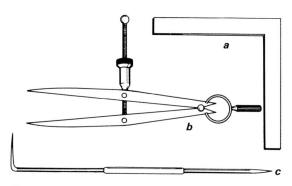

Illus. 46. Tools for tracing a design. *a.* steel square. *b.* dividers. *c.* tracing point.

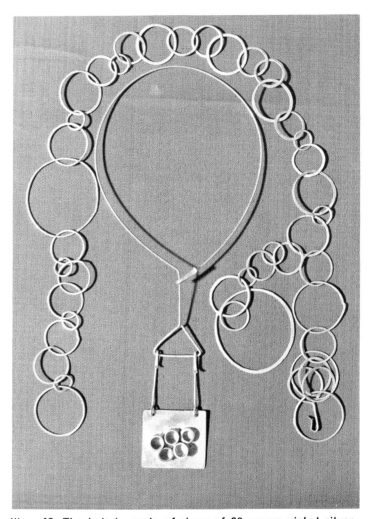

Illus. 48. The belt is made of rings of 20-gauge nickel-silver wire, shaped, flattened and soldered together after looping. The necklace is made of 20-gauge hammer-hardened brass wire. The pendant is a piece of copper to which were soldered small copper rings. These rings were cut from the kind of copper tubing used in plumbing.

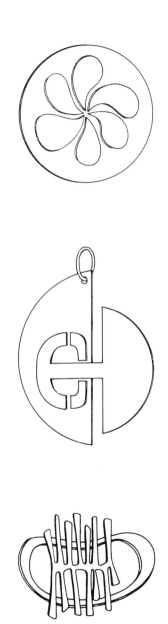

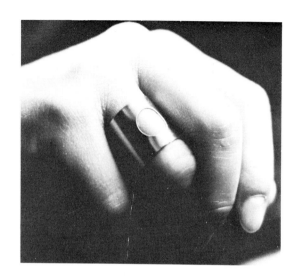

Cutting Out with Shears

The *straight shears* are used for cutting straight lines. The *circle-cutting shears* are for cutting curved lines. *Compound shears* are available also, at a higher price, but they require you to put forth less effort in cutting.

You must hold the blades of the shears parallel to the flat surface of the sheet of metal and perpendicular to the edge. Otherwise, the thin plate will slip between the blades, crushing it and damaging the tool (Illus. 51). The point of the circle-cutting shears should always be turned upwards (Illus. 52).

Cutting Out

Tools and Materials: Straight metal shears. Circle-cutting metal shears. Jeweler's saw. C-clamp. Small board. Hand drill and drill bits (for opening up inside cuts for the saw blade).

Measuring the Metal

You don't need a large piece of metal to make a piece of jewelry one inch long, so choose a size only a little bit larger all around than your design.

Cutting out can be done with metal shears or the jeweler's saw. The shears are faster than the saw, but they tend to deform the metal and require a certain amount of physical strength. Try to measure and cut a piece of metal so that the left-overs have as regular a shape as possible for use in another project.

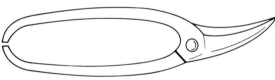

Illus. 50. Circle-cutting shears.

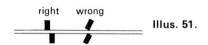

right wrong

Illus. 51.

Illus. 52.

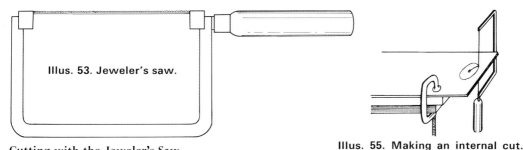

Illus. 53. Jeweler's saw.

Illus. 55. Making an internal cut.

Cutting with the Jeweler's Saw

Clamp the piece to be cut to the edge of the worktable with a small board and two C-clamps (Illus. 54). Do not lean heavily on the saw. Let the teeth bite lightly into the metal (Illus. 54). Unlike other kinds of saws, the teeth of the jeweler's saw point backwards, towards the handle, so that all cutting is done on the downstroke.

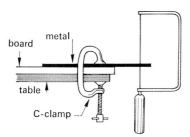

Illus. 54. Set-up for sawing.

Don't just jiggle the saw up and down—you might break the blade. Cut a downward stroke; draw the blade back a trifle so that it is not touching the metal and lift it; then make another downward stroke, and so on. If you rasp the teeth backward over the metal, you will quickly dull them.

If you want to cut out the middle of a piece (see ring in Illus. 49), begin by drilling a hole just large enough to pass the blade through, *teeth*

pointing downward, and clamp it again in the saw frame (Illus. 55).

If a piece of metal is pulled out of shape by cutting, you must flatten it out (Illus. 69).

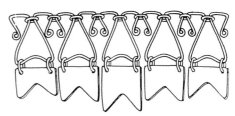

Illus. 56. A belt made of circles and rings.

Illus. 57. Sheet metal cut out to conform to the shape of the wire elements.

27

Illus. 58. This beautiful necklace is made of three pieces of chased nickel-silver (see page 39) and wire pendants with the ends flattened.

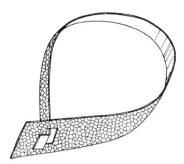

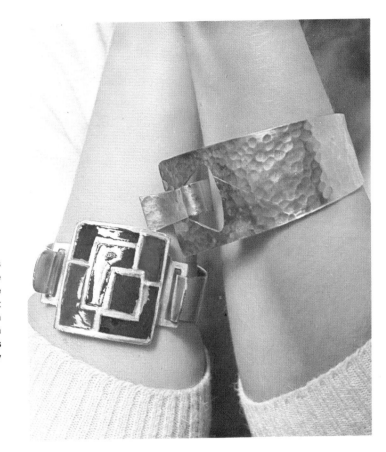

Illus. 59. Hammering produces lovely effects on sheet metal (see page 39) as you can see in the bracelet on the right. The bracelet on the left is made of copper with strips of nickel-silver soldered on to form a design. To enamel pieces such as these, use easy-to-apply "cold enamel."

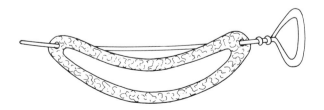

29

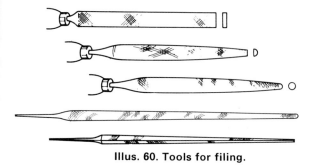

Illus. 60. Tools for filing.

Filing

Tools and Materials: Bench vice. Sheets of lead or wooden blocks to face the rough jaws of the vice. Flat file, round file, half-round file, all semi-fine. Fine round file (called a "rat-tail"). Fine, triangular (three-square) file. Emery cloth.

The purpose of filing is to finish the work of the saw or the shears, removing the burr from the edges of the metal and correcting the imperfections of the cut. You will need not only semi-fine flat, half-round, or round files, but, in addition, very fine needle files, which will permit you to file out the smallest indentation. Needle files come in sets, containing all useful shapes for the jeweler's purpose.

Grip the workpiece in the vice, placing between the metal and each jaw of the vice a piece of wood or lead to protect it (Illus. 61). Jaw covers can be made from fairly thin sheet lead and left permanently in place. This is better than trying to juggle three separate pieces between the vice-jaws without dropping them. If the pieces to be filed have a simple shape, you can do just as well by holding the workpiece in one hand and filing with the other.

The edge to be filed should not project more than $\frac{1}{8}''$ or $\frac{1}{4}''$ above the vice-jaws. If it sticks up too high, the metal will vibrate and be distorted (Illus. 62). If you place it too low, you run the risk of filing the vice.

Place the flat side of the file on the edge of the metal you are about to attack, at a 45° angle to the edge. File with the full length of the toothed blade. Alternate filing from left to right and from right to left. Apply enough pressure to the file to cause the teeth to bite into the metal, but keep the pressure steady at all times so as to avoid filing irregularities into the edge (Illus. 63).

Finish the job by smoothing the edges with emery cloth. Cut this into small pieces, about 2″ square for easy handling.

Try to work only the edge of the metal and avoid scratching the surface. Following filing, the edge should feel perfectly smooth when you run a finger along it.

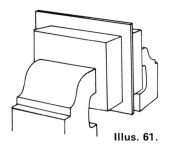

Illus. 61.

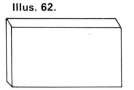

Illus. 62.

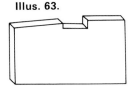

Illus. 63.

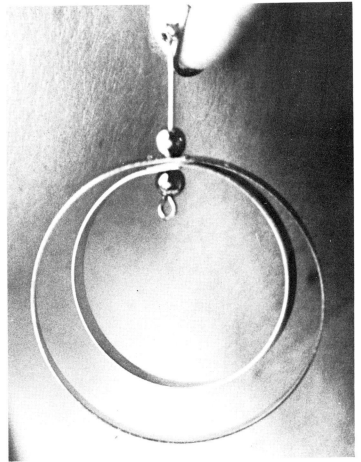

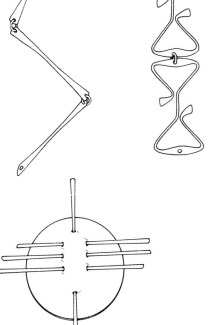

Piercing

Tools and Materials: Grease pencil. Center punch. Ball-peen hammer. C-clamp. Wooden board. Hand drill. Three drill bits of high-speed steel, numbers 60, 55, and 52 (these come in a set). Square-pointed reamer. Round needle file.

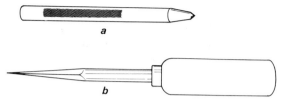

Illus. 65. Tools for piercing. *a*. center punch. *b*. square-pointed reamer.

Piercing allows you to make holes in the sheet metal necessary for passing jump rings and rivets through. First, mark the point to be pierced with a grease pencil; then mark it plainly and precisely with the center punch, lightly tapping it with the hammer. Clamp the workpiece to a wooden board with a C-clamp.

Choose a drill bit slightly larger in diameter than that of the wire of which the jump ring is made and smaller than, or equal to, the size of any rivet you might be using. Insert the bit into the hand drill, place the point on the punch mark, and start drilling. Turn the handle *slowly and put little or no pressure* on the drill. Such bits as these are very tiny and break easily. It is highly important that you always hold the drill perfectly perpendicular to the metal plate (Illus. 66).

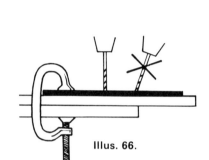

Illus. 66.

Do not let the piece be held by a "helping hand." If the bit should break, you could not prevent the drill from jumping aside and plunging the remainder of the broken bit through a "friendly finger." Once the hole is drilled, you can enlarge it with the reamer if necessary (Illus. 67); then remove the burr with a round needle file.

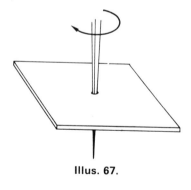

Illus. 67.

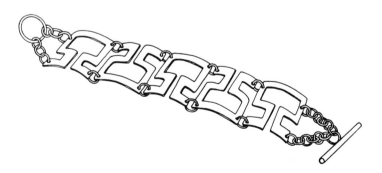

Illus. 68. A variety of techniques can produce all of the pieces shown here—flattening, piercing, soldering, bending. If you choose to enamel some of your pieces, use "cold enamel."

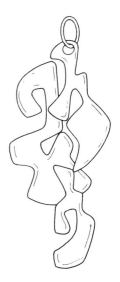

33

Flattening

Tools: Wooden bench block. Steel bench anvil. Flat-faced hammer.

Flattening is necessary when a piece has been deformed by cutting or by any other cause. Place it on the steel anvil and cover it with a block of wood. If one surface has been hammered or chiselled for texture, that face should be in contact with the wood.

Hammer on top of this sandwiched assembly until the piece held between the two plane surfaces is straightened or flattened out. Where very small pieces are concerned, you can bring them back into shape by tapping directly on them with the flat-faced hammer. In such a case, you must strike with the face perfectly flat (Illus. 69). Actually, you are far better off using a rawhide hammer for this. Rawhide hammers are available in various sizes from a craft supply house. The rawhide hammer will not mark the workpiece as the steel hammerface is likely to do.

Illus. 70. This graceful cup shape was accomplished by the technique of "bumping up."

Bumping Up

Tools: Ball (forming) hammer. Planishing hammer, or, ball-peen hammer. Metal block or bench anvil. Soldering torch. Wood block. Dividers. Circle-cutting shears. Semi-fine file.

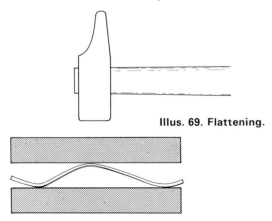

Illus. 69. Flattening.

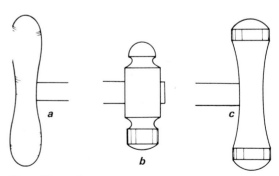

Illus. 71. *a.* forming hammer. *b.* ball-peen hammer. *c.* planishing hammer.

Bumping up is the operation that makes a metal plate concave on one side and convex on the other. Both happen simultaneously, of course. It involves two operations: Beating in and beating out. Let's make a small cup to experiment with this technique.

First, trace a circle with dividers of the desired diameter and cut it out of 22- or 20-gauge copper with the circle-cutting shears. Dress down the circumference with a semi-fine file.

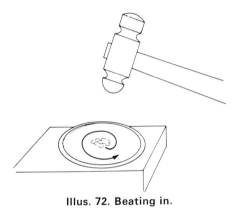

Illus. 72. Beating in.

Beating In: Take the copper circle in your hand and place it on the steel bench anvil. Strike four or five blows in the middle of it with the ball side of the ball-peen hammer (Illus. 72).

Starting from the edge of this central hammering, hammer the copper along a spiral line that "unrolls" all the way to the edge (Illus. 72).

Since hammering hardens the metal considerably, next heat it red-hot with the torch; then cool it in a bucket of water. Then, you will be able to hollow out your little cup deeply by beating out.

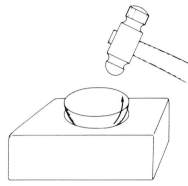

Illus. 73. Beating out.

Beating Out: First, you must hollow out a depression in a thick piece of wood. The depression should be shaped like a skullcap and be about 5″ across and $\frac{3}{8}$″ to $\frac{3}{4}$″ deep. Place the beaten-in and annealed piece in this depression. Then, with the ball end of the ball-peen, start striking the metal, starting at the middle (Illus. 73). As soon as a wrinkle shows up in the metal, wipe it out by hammering from the base of the fold, working towards the edge.

If the cup is not deep enough and the metal becomes too hard for working, start the whole procedure over again—beating in, annealing, and beating out.

When the cup is finally hollowed out enough to suit you, get rid of the irregularities in shape and the little bumps left from hammering by working with a planishing hammer on a wooden bench block, taking care that each blow of the hammer strikes with the face *flat* against the metal.

Now, you can re-cut the edge of the cup to straighten it out, if necessary, or file it until it is flat and smooth.

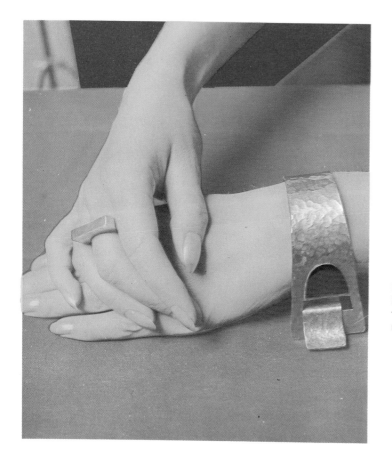

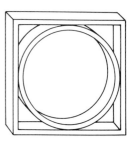

Illus. 74. A unique ring made from heavy sheet brass, cut out with the jeweler's saw, and a bracelet made of 20-gauge brass, hammered and bent.

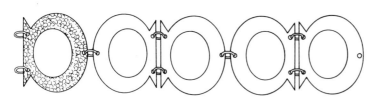

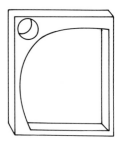

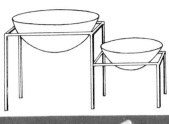

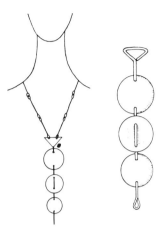

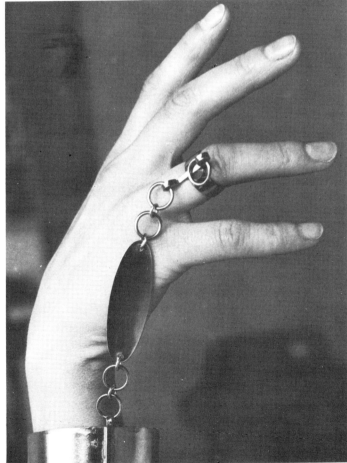

Illus. 75. The bumping-up technique was used here to create the large element connecting the ring and the bracelet.

Illus. 76. A piece of sheet brass bent into a bracelet is adorned with strips of wire soldered on to form a design.

jaws more closely). Adjust the metal plate between the angles in such a manner that the bending line appears just above the level of the angle (Illus. 77). Always grip the shortest side of the bend in the vice-jaws to give you more bending leverage with the long side. Gently bend the plate over by hand.

Finish by hammering along the bend with the flat face of the hammer. Strike first at one end, then at the other, working the hammer blows towards the middle (Illus. 77).

To avoid damaging the plate with hammer marks, protect it with a thick rag.

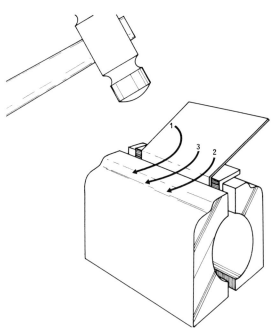

Illus. 77. Bending sheet metal.

Bending

Tools: Graduated steel ruler. Tracing point. Bench vice. Angle irons to go between the jaws of the vice. Planishing hammer.

With tracing point and ruler, mark the line along which the plate is to be bent. Place the two angle irons between the jaws of the vice (for bending light-gauge metals, aluminum angles will work just as well and, as the inside corners are square instead of rounded, they will fit the vice-

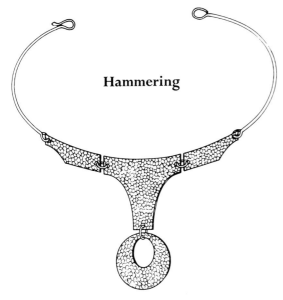

Hammering

Illus. 78. A hammered necklace.

regulate the force of the hammer blows—heavy enough to produce the effect desired, and even enough to make all the facets the same. However, be sure also to hammer the edges of the piece more lightly to avoid deforming them.

Illus. 79. Hammering.

Tools: Ball (forming) hammer, ball-peen hammer, or hammer and dapping punch.

Hammering consists of covering the surface of the plate with tiny facets, or hammer marks. This technique gives an attractive, antique look to the metal, and also gives you a chance to hide scratches and the ugly kind of hammer marks that are applied accidentally!

Hold the metal on the steel bench anvil with one hand and strike it with the ball of the hammer with the other. If you want to get the smallest of small facets, use a dapping punch and a hammer. Do not let the facets overlap. You must also

Chasing

Tools: Flat-face hammer. Various punches, dapping punches, and chasing tools. Flat block of lead or soft wood.

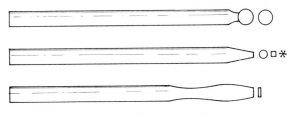

Illus. 80. Chasing tools.

Chasing is a rather delicate operation and requires a good deal of care. You can buy ready-

39

made punches, or you can make them yourself from large nails or spikes, filed or ground to the desired shape. You can buy small chisels and ball-headed dapping punches at a jeweler's supply house.

To hold the workpiece, drive three nails into the block of wood or lead, as shown in Illus. 81. Make the impressions in the metal by tapping the punches, chisels or dapping punches with a hammer. Hold the punch perpendicular to the metal plate and strike it with a sharp blow of the hammer (Illus. 81).

Illus. 82. Chasing gives this belt buckle a medieval look.

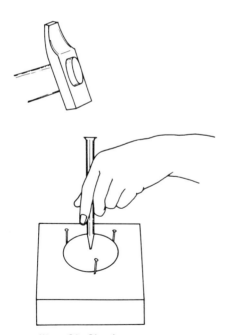

Illus. 81. Chasing.

Riveting

Riveting consists of joining two plates of metal together by means of rivets. A rivet is a kind of unpointed nail fixed in position by hammering.

Tools and Materials: Grease pencil. Center punch. Hand drill. Drill bits of the correct size for the rivets. Square-pointed reamer. Metal-cutting shears or a jeweler's saw. Bench vice. Planishing (or ball-peen) hammer. Rivets. Riveting-snap (a tool having a cup-shaped depression in one end for forming rivet heads).

There are three kinds of rivets: Buttonhead (roundhead), panhead (flat), and counter-sunk head (Illus. 83). Because of their decorative

Illus. 83. Rivets. *a.* buttonhead. *b.* panhead.
c. countersunk.

qualities, the buttonheads are most suitable for use in jewelry-making (Illus. 84).

The rivets can be of copper or steel; however, aluminum rivets are also available.

Setting Out

Mark the location for the rivet first with grease pencil, and then with the center punch, on the metal plate that is to be on top. Then drill a hole. Mark the bottom piece to be attached through the drilled hole. In some cases, both pieces can be clamped together and drilled simultaneously. The holes should be of the same diameter as, or of a diameter slightly smaller than, that of the rivet. Where necessary, the holes can be reamed a trifle with the square-pointed reamer.

Rivets come in various lengths and you should be able to get hold of a length just right for your work. The end of the rivet should project above the work no higher than the length of its own diameter. If it does, cut off the excess with the cutting pliers.

Riveting with the Hammer

Grip the riveting-snap in the bench vice. The hollow in the end of the snap is turned upwards, of course, and you snuggle the rivet head into it. This will keep the round head from becoming flattened. Hold the work absolutely horizontal, perpendicular to the vertical snap—otherwise, you may mar the work.

With a planishing hammer or the flat face of a ball-peen hammer, strike a vertical blow smartly on the end of the projecting rivet (Illus. 85). This will bulge it and hold the pieces firmly together. Do not hammer too hard, but continue hammering from all sides so that the crushed metal

Illus. 84. Buttonhead rivets are used here to produce a unique pendant.

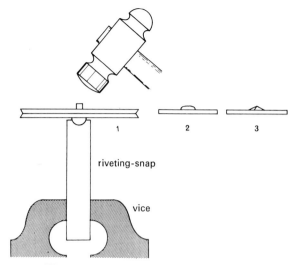

Illus. 85. Riveting with the hammer.

The simplest metals for you to work on are zinc and copper. Copper is harder than zinc and produces finely etched lines, while zinc will give you coarser lines.

There are certain precautions you must observe when etching. First, *acid is always added slowly to water*, and never vice versa. Keep this in mind at all times. If you must add more water to a solution, pour the additional water into an empty glass container. Then *add the solution to it*.

Be sure to work near an open window and keep fumes out of your eyes. If acid or fumes get in your eyes, flush immediately with water, and call a doctor.

Keep a tray of clear water near the etching tray for rinsing your fingers. If acid touches your skin, hold the affected spot under running water for at least 15 minutes. The best thing is to wear finger sheaths for protection. These are better than rubber gloves because gloves are awkward and sometimes slippery and you might drop the acid.

Always use separate solutions for each metal, and store acids or dilute baths in glass bottles having glass or plastic tops. Be sure to *label* each bottle.

expands and begins to round off (Illus. 85). Then, with care, continue hammering until you have shaped the end of the rivet into a pyramid with four sides (Illus. 85).

The riveting will be spoiled if you strike too hard, or if the projecting end of the rivet was too long.

Etching

Basically, etching with acid consists of the very thin hollowing-out of a design in metal by means of the metal-dissolving action of the acid. A resist is first applied to the metal, and then the design worked with an etching needle. The metal is placed in an acid bath which etches the exposed design, leaving the remainder untouched.

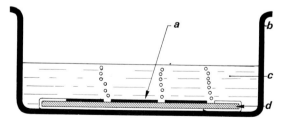

Illus. 86. Etching. *a*. design being etched. *b*. glass or plastic container. *c*. acid. *d*. metal piece.

42

Illus. 87. These designs are etched into copper, zinc, and brass. Once the metal has been cleaned and polished, the designs will come to life.

Tools and Materials: Emery cloth. Black asphaltum varnish, acid resist or 4-lb. cut shellac. Stove polish (available at hardware dealer). Soft brush. Graphite. Scraper. Hydrochloric acid for zinc. Mineral spirits (paint thinner). Plastic or glass bowls or trays. Metal polish. 70% nitric acid for copper-type metals. Single-edged razor blades, utility knives, needlepoint scribers. Tongs.

Etching Zinc

Take the piece you wish to etch and de-grease the surface by a thorough scrubbing with a detergent. Follow this with a gentle abrasive such as fine, powdered pumice.

With a camel's hair brush, coat the back side of the piece and the edges with the resisting

medium. If you use shellac, apply two or three coats.

Paint the surface to be etched all over with stove polish and allow to dry. Apply two or three coats, letting each dry before applying the next. The surface should have a flat, black mat finish. When completely dry, trace your design on the surface by loading the back of the drawing to be traced with graphite. The graphite will be set off on the black surface as light lines.

Then, using needlepoint scribers for thin lines and utility knives or razor blades for large areas, scrape the design out carefully, following the graphite outline.

In preparing the acid bath, begin with a weak solution, say, 1 part acid to 5 parts water. *Put the*

43

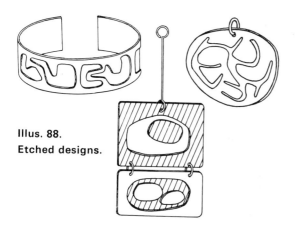

**Illus. 88.
Etched designs.**

water in the container first. Then add the acid. Never fill the container to the top so as to avoid splashing or overflowing. You can easily tell if you have put in too much acid because the bubbles on the plate that will arise because of the chemical reaction will be big and part of the resist will be removed. When you have become more expert, you can use a stronger acid solution than at first, since, as you will discover, the weaker the solution, the longer the etching process. *However, the water content must always be greater than the acid.*

To check how well the etching is going, touch the edge of an etched area with the needlepoint scriber. Keep on until the design is bitten in as deeply as you want it. Remember the acid will bite sideways as well as downward, so expect that the lines of your design will be somewhat wider than your original tracing.

When the piece is etched to your satisfaction, remove it from the acid with *tongs.* Hold it under running water to wash off the chemical. Then clean it with paint thinner to remove the stove

polish. Polish the unetched surface with a good metal polish.

Etching Copper-type Metals

Read the section on zinc first.

After you have cleaned the copper piece thoroughly, paint the back side of the metal with black asphaltum varnish or 4-lb. cut shellac and let dry. Trace the design on the metal using carbon paper. Then scratch the outlines into the metal with a scriber. Clean by washing thoroughly with a detergent, and rinse in running water. Allow to dry completely.

With a small red sable brush, carefully paint the piece around the outlines of the design with asphaltum varnish or two coats of the shellac, leaving open the areas to be etched. If the paint tends to flow too freely, thicken it with lampblack (available at your hardware dealer). In any case, lampblack powder in the shellac will darken it and make it easier to see on the metal surface.

Again, in preparing your acid bath (in this case nitric acid) begin with a weak solution. Nitric acid is more powerful than hydrochloric acid, but the copper is harder, so try the same 5 parts water to 1 part acid until you are familiar with the effects. In any case, *never* use more than 3 parts acid to 5 of water.

Place the water in the container first. Slowly add the acid. Lay the metal in the bath. Check the action by using the point of a scriber to lift the piece carefully. (Be careful not to splash when lowering back into the acid.) When you are satisfied with the etching, remove with tongs, and rinse in running water. Clean with paint thinner or turpentine, and then polish.

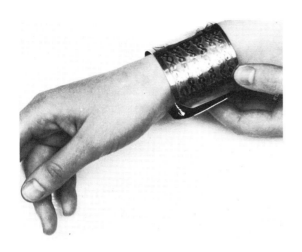

Finishing

Cleaning and Polishing

Materials: Soft abrasive, such as kitchen cleanser. Metal polish. Clean, soft rags. Clear, mat, brushing lacquer for metal. Soft brush.

You must always begin cleaning by flushing the workpiece with a large quantity of running water. Then, you can use ordinary kitchen cleanser on a slightly damp rag. However, it is preferable to use the kind of polishing paste used by automotive body builders. Emery cloth should *not* be used at this stage because it will scratch the metal. You can also use whiting, which is pow-

dered chalk, on a damp rag, but wash off the residue thoroughly.

Polishing is done with a metal polish you can buy at your hardware dealer's. Apply with a soft cloth, let dry, and polish well with a dry cloth.

If you prefer a dull finish to a bright, shiny one, do the cleaning with a piece of sliced lemon or wood ashes; then polish with floor wax. Powdered pumice rubbed on with a damp rag will also result in a mat finish.

Jewelry pieces made of metal sheet and wire tarnish quickly unless properly protected from moisture and harmful gases in the air. To protect such pieces, mix clear brushing lacquer with an equal quantity of lacquer thinner in a glass jar. Fasten the jewelry piece to a short length of wire, dip it in the lacquer, and hold it above the surface to drain. Then, hang it up by hooking the upper end of the dipping wire over a drying line on the edge of a table.

The thin, fluid lacquer will continue to run down the piece and collect in a drop hanging from the lowermost edge. Touch this drop from beneath with a toothpick, and the lacquer will instantly flow down the toothpick. Wipe it off on a rag, and continue touching the spot until the lacquer ceases to form a drop. Continue with all the pieces ready to be finished.

In fifteen or twenty minutes, you can apply a second coat in the same way to the first piece. Three or four coats are enough.

Patinas

A blue-green patina on copper:
Dissolve together:
4 teaspoonfuls of distilled water
3 teaspoonfuls of ammonium carbonate
1 teaspoonful of sal ammoniac
Apply with a brush. The patina will appear within a few hours.

A clear, grey patina on copper:
Brush perchloride of iron on the piece. When the desired tone is reached, stop the reaction by washing in running water.

Iridescent patina on copper:
The propane gas torch will cause a moiré pattern to appear in blues, pinks and greens for a very handsome effect. To preserve the effect, rub the surface with oil as soon as the colors show up. You could also spread soap over the surface; then polish it with a piece of newsprint (newspaper that has not been printed on).

Greyish-black patina in the hollows:
Rub dry, powdered soap into the depressions. Turn the propane gas flame on it until the soap melts; then polish with newsprint.

A bronzelike patina:
Rub the piece with a little *used* crankcase oil. Heat, then polish. The bronze particles in the oil (from the auto bearings) stick to the piece. You can get the same effect by using any kind of oil into which a little bronzing powder has been stirred. Bronzing powder is available at paint shops in different shades.

A tin patina:
Flow a little soft solder (or pure tin) on the piece and rub it off with a rag while still hot, so as to leave only traces of tin on the surface.

Illus. 90. All kinds of objects can be mounted on your finished jewelry. Here, two pebbles were cemented together and then mounted on a simple rod of square nickel-silver, shaped and hammered on the end.

Mounting

There are numerous jeweler's accessories, called findings, for sale in hobby shops and at jewelers' supply houses, which you can use to mount jewelry pieces. These include: earclips or earring screw-backs; pin findings for brooches; cuff-links findings.

To mount a metal piece of one of these, simply soft-solder it on (page 17). You can even solder on an enamelled piece, as the heat of fusion of the solder is very low compared to that of the enamel, so you cannot melt the latter. You will, of course, have to re-polish the surfaces after soldering. It is possible to use a metal cement that comes in a tube. Follow directions scrupulously.

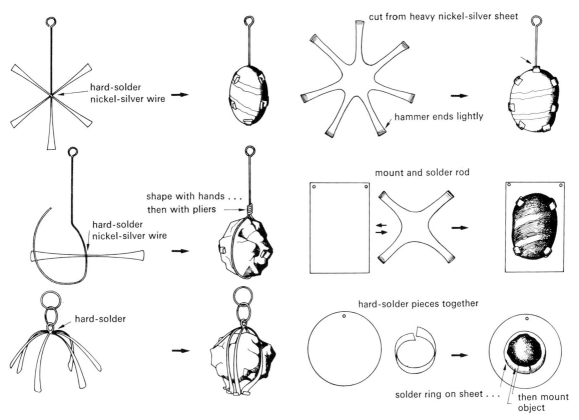

cut from heavy nickel-silver sheet

hard-solder
nickel-silver wire

hammer ends lightly

shape with hands . . .
then with pliers

mount and solder rod

hard-solder
nickel-silver wire

hard-solder

hard-solder pieces together

solder ring on sheet . . .   then mount
object

Illus. 91. Mounting accessories on your jewelry. Natural materials such as stones, shells, and dried nuts enhance the elegance of your hand-wrought designs.

Index